COPING WITH CHAOS

COPING
WITH CHAOS

Brian Cambourne
Jan Turbill

Distributed in the U.S.A.
by
HEINEMANN EDUCATIONAL BOOKS, INC.
70 Court Street
Portsmouth, New Hampshire 03801

PRIMARY ENGLISH TEACHING ASSOCIATION

ISBN 0 909955 66 2
Dewey 372.6
First published February 1987
Reprinted 1988
Copyright © Primary English Teaching Association 1987
PO Box 167 Rozelle NSW 2039 Australia
Design consultant: Mark Jackson
Editor: J. V. Steele
Cover design based on plate VI, 1st state, from
G.B. Piranesi, *Invenzioni capric di Carceri* (c. 1745)
Typeset in 11/12 Caledonia by Dovatype
Printed by Australian Print Group, Maryborough, Vic.

Contents

Acknowledgement

This book has evolved over several years. It began as a research project by members of the Centre for Studies in Literacy from the University of Wollongong. The project team watched seven Kindergarten classrooms in action in Cringilla, Nareena Hills, Lake Illawarra South and Warrawong Public Schools. Since then we have observed many teachers and their children in classrooms in New South Wales, Victoria and Queensland. More recently we have been particularly involved in Pleasant Heights, Figtree, Balarang and Hampen Park Public Schools.

This book could never have been written without the generosity of the teachers and children in all of these schools. The teachers were willing for us to come into their classrooms and be part of the 'furniture' as we observed them and their children in action. The data collected has formed the basis of the thinking in this book. We have simply put into writing what is really going on in these classrooms. We are extremely grateful to the teachers and children for providing us with such opportunities.

DEDICATED
to all the kids
who gave us
the privilege of
watching them learn

CHAPTER ONE
Setting the Scene

Brian Cambourne was running the final session of a one-day inservice course at a Department of Education Professional Services Centre. In a carpeted seminar room thirty or more teachers sat in a semi-circle, all facing the front. Cambourne recalls it this way:

> As a finale to the day's course I'd been conducting, I decided to show a videotape which I thought was a good demonstration of a typical, so-called 'process-writing' classroom in action. Towards the end of the video I heard: '*It looks like unstructured, uncoordinated, unmanageable chaos. The kids are all over the place. "Confusion writing" would be a better name for it.*'
>
> The comment was made by an experienced infants teacher sitting towards the front. On the surface, her comment was directed at a colleague who was sitting nearby. However, it was made in one of those stage whispers which penetrate to the farthest corners of a room, and so everyone, especially me, could hear it. It was really a comment directed at the whole fabric of the course which I'd just run. Obviously she was unhappy with what I'd presented and she was letting me know. As far as she was concerned, there was no validity in what I'd been advocating. She was not convinced that the principles I'd been describing could *ever* work. On the contrary, if I'd pushed her, I'm certain she would have told me that 'learning could never occur in the midst of all that confusion'.
>
> At the time I was irritated and a little angered by this thinly disguised rejection of what I'd presented in the course, but coward that I am, I pretended not to have heard. But I did, and that comment sent me away thinking about how I could demonstrate the learning that *was* taking place in the apparent chaos. Just how do children and teachers cope with these learning settings?

Let's examine this short episode carefully, as the comment made by this teacher was a fair one. Someone with traditional views on how writing should be taught to very young children must find it difficult to tease out what precisely is going on in these classrooms. Children do appear to be 'all over the place'. The noise level, both from the talk and from the chairs scraping, feet moving and pencils tapping, *does* seem high—especially when magnified by the unselective nature of the video sound recording system. It *does* seem like confusing, rowdy mayhem. Furthermore there *is* a lot of seemingly uncontrolled movement and talk in the room.

What are these children doing?

- Children seem to be talking to whom they please, whenever they please.
- Some children appear to be arguing about words and letters.
- Some appear to be wandering from their seats, whenever they please, to every corner of the room. They are looking at the wall charts, either alone, in pairs or in larger groups, and discussing what is written on them.
- Some are perusing books.
- Some appear to be disturbing their peers who *are* engaged in writing, and asking questions like: 'Shelley, SHELLEY! How do you write a "b-uh"?'
- Some are drawing pictures.
- Some are reading texts which they've created to anyone who will listen; a few are staring into space.
- Some are re-reading audibly, to no one in particular, texts which they are currently creating.
- Some appear to be quietly engaged in the act of writing (i.e. making marks on paper with a pencil).
- The majority appear to be doing whatever they please.

Amid this apparent turmoil the teacher appears to be conducting friendly chats with individual children, seemingly oblivious to the chaos surrounding her. And while the term 'chaos' may be a little strong, there is certainly a distinct lack of the kind of 'order' which has been a feature of Australian classrooms for as long as most of us can remember.

Why are the children doing what they are doing?

The classroom captured on this videotape is not all that unusual. In fact it is typical of what is happening in many infants classrooms in Australia, partly as a consequence of dissatisfaction with traditional ways of teaching young learners to read and write, and partly as a consequence of the new vision of learning to write which Donald Graves has promoted. Since his first visit to Australia in 1980, there has been a minor revolution in the way writing and, more recently, reading are being taught to children in the early grades. More and more infants classrooms have been attempting to implement the principles which Graves (1983) espouses. Because his work emphasises the processes involved in writing, it has become known in Australia as 'process writing'.

Generally Graves' work has been favourably received. Many who have been exposed to his work have been enthused by what he describes, often arguing it is 'just plain common sense'. There have been many attempts to replicate it, and local research literature is replete with data drawn from descriptions of the results of implementing it. Indeed, his work has been so persuasive that some State departments have rewritten their curriculum policies in order to capture the essence of his approach to the teaching and learning of writing.

So why another book on writing?

While in recent years much has been written to advance our knowledge of how young children actually put marks on paper and gradually work their way towards becoming literate, there have been relatively few attempts to focus at a more macroscopic level, the classroom level, and to document how young learners respond to the kind of learning contexts which result from implementing 'process-writing' principles. Previous research has focused on individual learners. We intend to widen the scope and 'zoom out' to focus on the whole class setting, since there is a strong need to examine:

- how young learners respond to an environment which de-emphasises traditional, orderly, didactic, teacher-controlled methods
- what *kind* of learning strategies evolve and develop in children in 'process-writing' classrooms which lead them to make marks on paper and eventually to become literate
- whether these classrooms are really as 'chaotic' as they appear.

In this book we attempt to answer such questions by describing how young children from various cultural and linguistic backgrounds have responded to and coped with the conditions surrounding them in 'process-oriented' classrooms. We will describe the behaviours of children who were members of 'process-writing' classrooms and the conditions which were seen to exist in these rooms. We will examine the learning strategies the children developed as they attempted to solve the written language puzzle—that world of print out there in their environment.

In a later chapter we will discuss what this means in terms of two young children's writing development over a period of time. Finally we will discuss the broad implications this has for classroom teaching and organisation, so that the perceived 'chaos' can become a highly organised and successful centre of language learning.

Brian Cambourne records his observations in the classroom.

CHAPTER TWO

A Study of 'Process-Writing' Classrooms

An initial project was begun in 1982, when seven Kindergarten classrooms with children aged between 4.9 years and 5.9 years were regularly and systematically observed by a team of researchers from the University of Wollongong. Members of the team sat in class with the children, observing and recording their behaviours, interacting with them about their writing, collecting and analysing their writing products and talking with their teachers. In all classrooms there were children from both English-speaking backgrounds (ESB) and non-English-speaking backgrounds (NESB). Most of the latter group arrived in Kindergarten at the beginning of the year with very little understanding of English.

Since then both authors have continued to observe similar 'process-writing' classrooms in action from Kindergarten through to Year 6 (5–12 year olds), following the same information-gathering processes. We will draw on *all* this information in the following chapter.

'Process-writing' classrooms . . . What do they look like? What is common to them all?

Thus far the term 'process-writing' has always been written within inverted commas. This is because of the difficulty of specifying with any precision just what it means. What makes a classroom a 'process-writing' classroom? What are the identifying characteristics? What conditions exist in these 'process-oriented' classrooms?

When these questions were discussed with each of the teachers observed, they generally agreed that the essence of what they were attempting to implement was to be found in the writings of Walshe (1981), Graves (1983), Turbill (1982; 1983) and Butler & Turbill (1984). It also became obvious that each of them had different ideas on just how to establish their 'process classrooms'.

It was decided, in the initial project, to first try to identify any characteristics which were common to all seven Kindergarten classrooms. After careful observation of the contexts in which these seven teachers taught what they believed to be 'process writing', and with the support of many discussions with them, a set of conditions began to emerge which were characteristic of all classrooms in varying degrees. Subsequent classroom observations since 1982 have supported this model, shown in the table opposite.

If all these conditions are present in the classroom to a relatively high degree, then such a classroom may be labelled as a 'process-writing' setting or, for that matter, a 'process-oriented' setting. (In recent years the term 'whole language' setting has also become accepted.) The fact that these conditions could be identified in the classrooms observed did not mean the teachers used the terminology, or were even aware that such conditions did exist in their classrooms. Nor were the classrooms identical in every way. While at the overall level they were and are very similar with regard to each of the conditions, at the individual level there were subtle but important differences. Often these differences reflected the personality, background and professional development of the teachers.

For instance, in the case of *immersion*, the range of print items with which learners could readily and easily *engage* varied from classroom to classroom in both range and quality. In some classrooms the children were surrounded by a variety of commercial books, including big books, and by teacher/child-made books, teacher-made charts, children's writing, and posters from supermarkets and travel agencies; while in others only teacher-made wall charts were used and very few commercial or child/teacher-authored books were available. In one classroom there were over one thousand meaningful pieces of print on the walls, or hanging on strings criss-crossing the room and decorating the windows. In another there were less than one hundred.

Similarly the degree to which *responsibility* was implemented differed from teacher to teacher. One teacher, while permitting the children to take *responsibility* for what to write about and when to write, couldn't initially bring herself to allow them to take *responsibility* for *approximating* spellings. So, in the early part of the year, she gave all spellings to children on request. This consequently affected the degree to which the children *approximated* in their writing and were *engaged* in the process

CONDITIONS	HOW MANIFESTED IN THE CLASSROOM
Immersion in written medium	Print displays around room: labels, charts, books, dictated stories. Rooms can vary from high to low immersion.
Demonstration of how print medium is used	Reading print displays, choral reading, discussion of print and graphophonic conventions in context. Teacher demonstrations of how reading and writing are done. Regular opportunities to use print and see it being used. This condition can vary from many to few, and from functional to non-functional demonstration.
Expectations 'given off' by teacher to class	Positive/negative expectations which teachers hold and communicate (both implicitly and explicitly) to children and which affect their learning.
Responsibility for own learning	Degree to which the child is permitted to decide what will be written, when it will be written, what will be learned (from the demonstrations) and what will be ignored: e.g. which spelling convention will be mastered. This can vary from high to low.
Approximation: franchise to 'have a go'	Degree to which the child is allowed to approximate the adult model; degree to which emphasis is on error avoidance or error reduction. This can vary from high to low.
Practice: employing the developing skill	Degree to which opportunities to engage in writing-learning are made available. This can vary from high to low.
Engagement with the demonstrations made available	Degree to which the learner engages with print and the demonstrations being offered about how print works. This can vary from high to low, depending on the needs of the learner and the relevance of the print material and demonstrations to the learner.
Response: mutual exchanges between experts and novices	The type of response and the degree to which it is meaning-centred, non-threatening, functional, and relevant to the child's needs.

of learning how to spell. By contrast, another teacher gave children full *responsibility* for the spelling of what they wanted to write in their pieces by refusing to supply conventional spellings. She *expected* them to *approximate* their spelling and gave them plenty of opportunity for *practice* and *engagement* by simply instructing them to 'have a go', 'find it on the wall', 'use a book', 'ask a friend', or 'do the best you can'. Similarly, the presence of the other conditions described on p.7 varied in all classrooms in which we have been involved. They were present, however, to a sufficient degree for all these rooms to be loosely described as 'process-writing' classrooms.

What do children do in these classrooms and does learning result?

How do children learn in these settings called 'process-writing' classrooms? The results of our observations indicate that when the conditions described are implemented, the young learners develop an unusually uniform set of responses to the demands made by their learning situation. A new range of strategies begins to emerge in the children's repertoire—a range pertinent to written language. These strategies are child-oriented, child-developed and child-controlled. They are a form of 'scaffold' erected by the children to support them in their attempts to learn literacy, to solve the literacy learning puzzle.

The concept of scaffolding was first introduced to language learning by Jerome Bruner to describe the 'supportive language interactions' between parent and child. Graves (1983, p.271) describes scaffolding as:

> the temporary structures the mother uses to adapt the child's language, gestures and activity. Scaffolding follows the contours of the child's growth. As a child grows, the scaffold changes, but the principles of change, of temporary structures, do not.

We believe the strategies used by children in process-writing classrooms are scaffolds in the sense that the children erect structures for themselves in order to facilitate the literacy learning they are grappling with at that particular time. These structures support them while they 'cope' with the learning unrest taking place in their heads as new learning occurs. Once children feel both confident and competent to deal with the particular part of the literacy puzzle they've been trying to solve, they will remove the scaffold. They will no longer use the strategy because the connections have been made; they have learnt that part of the literacy puzzle. Because children develop these strategies in order to grapple with, or cope with the language learning puzzle, we have called such strategies 'coping strategies'. While they may differ from child to child and class to class in terms of the intensity and frequency with which they are used, in our observations they were similar enough in kind to be easily and readily recognised. We have been able to identify six broad categories of coping strategies which children use:

- Use of related activities/Clayton strategy
- Use of environmental print
- Use of repetition
- Assistance from and interaction with other children
- Assistance from and interaction with the teacher
- Use of 'temporary' spelling.

Let us now examine each one in more detail.

Use of related activities

In this category the strategy most commonly used by young children is drawing. It is a kind of stand-by they use until a little more knowledge about the concepts and functions of print has been learned. Why is it that young children almost exclusively use drawing? We believe it is because they perceive drawing as allowing them to use the tools of writing (pencil/paper) in ways which they have already learned to some degree and with which they feel confident. Furthermore drawing is acceptable to the teacher and it does relate to constructing meaning.

It is also related to the demonstrations of reading that many children have already had with books. Young children are read stories orally and they match the story heard with illustrations seen. They perceive the meaning coming from the illustrations in the book rather than through the words. What they do as young writers is almost the reverse. They illustrate whilst composing the oral story. In many cases teachers will hear young children 'tell' their story as they draw it. Drawing helps the child compose meaning.

Five-year-old Jimmy had drawn what seemed like scribble in the middle of his page. When asked by the teacher what it was, Jimmy replied in his very gruff voice, 'Grass'.

> TEACHER: The grass is long, isn't it? What do you do when the grass gets long?
> JIMMY: Cut tt.
> TEACHER: What do you cut it with?
> JIMMY: Mower (*Jimmy picks up his pencil and draws a mower in the top corner of his page*).
> TEACHER: Oh, you have drawn the mower. Is it magic?
> JIMMY: No.
> TEACHER: Well, who uses the mower to cut the long grass in your house?
> JIMMY: Grandad (*Jimmy picks up his pencil and now draws Grandad in the bottom corner of his page*).
> TEACHER: Now tell me what your drawing is all about, Jimmy.
> JIMMY: When the grass gets long, Grandad cuts it with the mower.

Jimmy is not writing but he is using a related activity which allows him to meet the demands of the writing setting in which he finds himself. He is rehearsing meaning and discovering how to develop and sequence a story for an intended audience.

Older children use drawing to accompany writing. Eight-year-old Megan was writing about a witch. She had introduced the setting and her characters. And she had written the problem. But then it had all become too hard.

When she brought the piece of writing to the teacher, there at the beginning of chapter 2 was a little box in which she had drawn a very detailed picture. She had resorted to a strategy which allowed her to show what was happening rather than having to find the words to describe what had happened. It was cognitively easier for her and got the intended message across. Having drawn the solution to the problem in her narrative, she was able to write it more easily.

Nine-year-old Miguel spent much of one writing session drawing lines and drawing an elaborate heading. This he did with fancy letters and various colours. He was resorting to related activities because, as he told his teacher, 'I want to write about the excursion to Old Sydney Town but I don't know where to start'. The task was too demanding, and so he fell back on activities which he could manage and which were related to the writing task the other children were involved in.

Ten-year-old Jesse, a non-reader in Year 5, each day in Sustained Silent Reading used various related activities which allowed him to participate successfully in the class activity. He picked a book with which he knew he could simulate the intended or expected behaviour—one with plenty of pictures which he could use to create his own set meanings, or one with a few phrases that he could read—and he browsed and/or tried to create meaning with pictures.

This strategy seems to be applicable only to situations which are essentially individual and/or result in products which are individually 'owned'. Let's describe it as:

Coping by using a functionally related form of behaviour which I'm capable of employing, or the Clayton strategy[1]—a way of writing when I'm not really writing.

Using environmental print

This strategy involves the use of any print displays, such as wall charts, room labels, word cards, alphabet cards, other children's 'published' stories, commercial books, posters, dictionaries, and any other print material available to the children in the room. The following common forms of this strategy were evident from our data.

Random use of letters

This strategy is used mostly by young writers who have not yet begun to read. It too has several sub-categories.

a) The child copies letters from various places around the room, or simply writes a series of letters but makes no obvious attempt to place any meaning on this 'writing'. Trung, a five-year-old Vietnamese boy, copied all the letters from the end of his pencil; Ibrahim, sitting opposite Walid, copied Walid's name tag upside down and back to front. When asked what the writing said, neither boy made any attempt to discuss it, but both were keen to talk about the pictures they had drawn.

---

[1]'Clayton' is the brand name of a non-alcoholic drink which has the slogan: 'The drink you have when you are not having a drink'.

b) Four-year-old Heidi had drawn a large detailed picture of a dog. Down the side of her drawing was a series of random letters she had written. Asked by her teacher what her writing said, she replied, 'I don't know.'

TEACHER: Well, you wrote it.
HEIDI: I *know*. I can write but I can't read yet.

c) Five-year-old Manel had drawn a large fish in the middle of her page. She carefully copied the word 'fish' underneath. She then wrote a series of random letters across the page. When asked to read her 'writing' Manel traced her finger across the word 'fish' and then her letters, telling the following story: 'This is a big fish and he swim in the water and he eat people and the girl swim in the pool.' When she came to the end of her letters she simply returned her finger to 'fish' and continued with her story. She then picked up her pen and drew the girl swimming in the pool so that the fish couldn't 'eat her'.

The random copying classification was applied when there was no clear evidence that the learner-writer was engaged in anything but a pattern-copying exercise, almost as an act of drawing rather than writing. What does seem to be happening, however, is that the child does realise that letters are connected with writing, not drawing. The examples above also demonstrate the progression from letters being something to do with writing to letters are writing and they tell a story. But there is no attempt yet to match each word said with each letter or 'word' written.

Copying environmental print but giving it another meaning

This category was applied when the learner-writer copied some of the environmental print but gave it a meaning different from the conventional meaning of the words copied. One example of this was when five-year-old Poppi copied the following words from a wall chart in the room—LOOK AT THE VERY HUNGRY CATERPILLAR—but 'read' it as, LOOK AT ME I'M AT BALLET. She drew a textually appropriate picture of herself at ballet. When she read her writing she would look at the drawing rather than the writing. There was no effort to match each word she 'read' with the words she had written.

Copying lists of words which can be read but with no attempt at storyline

This category described a common behaviour by which children would carefully choose individual words that they could read from displays around the room. They would copy these down list-fashion with no attempt to make meaning. Usually these words could be read by the young author when requested, but occasionally the author needed to refer to the original environmental source in order to identify the word. Shelley listed 22 different words from around the room with the drawing below. She was able to tell an oral story about her drawing which the teacher listened to with interest but made no attempt to scribe for her.

Copying labels from around the room and drawing the appropriate picture, or drawing a picture and copying the appropriate label

Five-year-old Donna looked around the room and then drew a house. Above it she copied the word 'house' from a chart on the wall. She looked

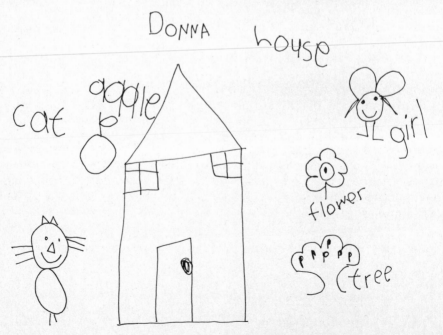

around again and drew a cat. She wrote 'cat'. This process continued until she had six items on her page. She then read her labels to anyone who would listen.

Copying words which can be read and constructing a storyline from them

Children exposed to *Breakthrough to Literacy* (Longman Cheshire, 1972) often use this strategy. Six-year-old Ali carefully chose words one at a time from the Breakthrough Teacher's Stand. He took each one back to his desk and carefully copied it onto his page. He returned each to the Stand before taking the next. He wrote: 'My home is big. My home is little. The boy is home'. Although Ali was composing written language and could read it, he was choosing words he could read and 'forcing' meaning with them.

Five-year-old Shelley, on the other hand, used the environmental print in a far more complex manner. She found words which she could read from around the room and then wove them into a semantically appropriate story line, producing the following text.

The cognitive processing that took place when this was observed was staggering in its complexity and intensity. It demonstrated the potential that very young children have for persevering with and concentrating on tasks for extended periods of time. It also reflects an obsession with correctness (see pp.26–27).

Copying environmental print to fulfil a specific function

This strategy is used particularly by older children. They scrounge words and ideas from wall charts around the room and from books they've been read or read themselves; they search reference books for what they need. This search tactic fulfils a specific function for the child.

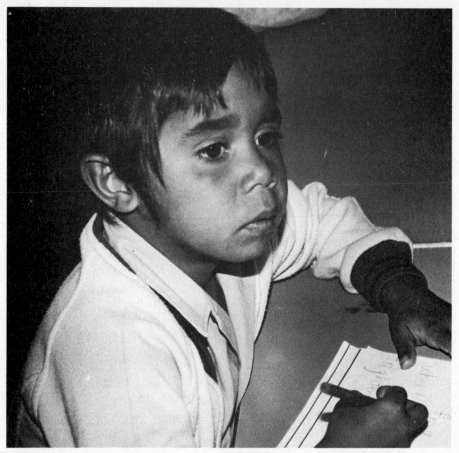

Scrounging the needed word from environmental print.

Nine-year-old Scott was writing about his experience on the 'pirate ship' at an amusement park. He had written:

> . . . We went right up in the air and were upside down. It was scary. I screamed.

He underlined 'scary' and got up to fetch *The Witches* by Roald Dahl, which was being read to them by the teacher. He flicked through the pages. Finding the page he'd been searching for, he took his pen, crossed out 'scary' and wrote 'terrifying', and then after 'screamed' he added: 'and panicked, quivering with fear'. He continued with: 'When we stopped I was trembling. My face was ashy and grey. I'd never do that again!' His piece now read:

> . . . We went right up in the air and were upside down. It was terrifying. I screamed and panicked, quivering with fear. When we stopped I was trembling. My face was ashy and grey. I'd never do that again!

Scott told his teacher he wanted 'scary' words and he remembered hearing them in the last part of the story she had read to them, and so he went specifically searching for them.

The differing way in which these categories are used by ESB and NESB children is interesting. The NESB children, particularly those in their first year of school, use *random copying* and *copying of words and labels* for a much longer period of time than the ESB children. Some NESB children we observed used this strategy up to their tenth month in school, until they had gained a certain level of control of the semantic system of English. Until this control ocurs, it seems, they are restricted to copying 'shapes' or 'patterns' which have little or no meaning to them. They must wait until they gain control of some meanings in English before they can move to copying labels and words around the room to which they can add some meaning. (It's worth noting, however, that the process of drawing and attempting some 'writing' gives these children many opportunities to practise and extend their oral language in non-threatening situations.)

The context in which any of these categories is used, whether by the very young child or the older writer, has the following characteristics: a task which must be done and which the learner has decided is worth doing; a significant other, usually the teacher, who expects it to be done; and some artefacts (charts, books, labels) which the learner knows have the imprimatur of the teacher and which contain demonstrations of the knowledge the learner needs. Thus we could describe this strategy as:

Coping by consciously scrounging from an artefact which has the imprimatur of authority and demonstrates what we need, and which we hope will become internalised for later use.

Use of repetition

This strategy involved the occurrence of the same picture items, the same set of letters, the same sentence portion, the same sentence, the same theme or topic, or the same genre or register on at least four occasions.

Repetition of picture items

Four-year-old Doan produced balloons: a 'papa balloon', a 'mama balloon' and a 'baby balloon'. The colour of the balloons changed but for two weeks she drew balloons. She would then touch each one and tell her teacher the English words. Needless to say, 'The Three Bears' was a major theme in the classroom at the time. Doan had learnt these English words and felt safe in being able to talk about them, and thus she continued to draw them.

Some children would draw the same items in their pictures for several months. Five-year-old Ivanka produced the same pictorial themes for seven months. They included a house with a TV aerial, flowers, a boy, a girl, and a stylised sun.

Repetition of letter groupings

This occurred when children repeated letter groupings which were related either to the specific letters making up their names or to letters from their siblings' names. The category also included NESB children who used letters from their first language. The boundary between this strategy and the *random use of environmental print* is hazy and they are in many ways very similar. But children who repeat letter groupings seem to have a set of letters in their heads which they use. They don't need to copy them from around the room. Five-year-old Norman constantly rearranged the letters in his name to produce new 'words'. He demonstrated a knowlege of one-to-one correspondence and that words give information to the reader. For example:

I Nmo man the moRAn to nrm rnm Nomr Nomn

I went to the dentist to get my teeth fixed.

With NESB children there was a tendency to repeat letters which were the same shape as those in their name. ZANA, whose name is comprised of letters which are mainly straight, produced what appeared to be a random string of straight letters—A, K, L, Z, K, I, T, N—and very few with curves in them—O, C, Q, P, R, U, D, B.

Five-year-old Mohamed wrote letters, rows of them, which looked more like Arabic than English, but had little relationship to any real Arabic letters. Mohamed could not speak sufficient English to 'read' his writing to us but would 'read' it in Arabic to his peers or to the Arabic ethnic aide.

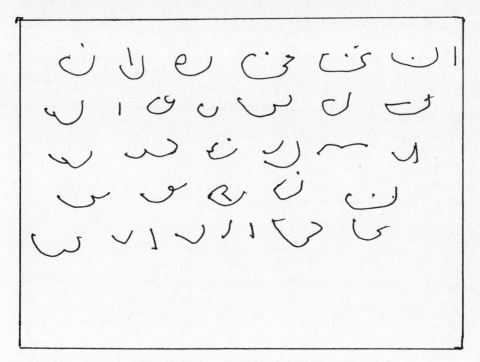

Repetition of whole sentences or sentence portions

This is exemplified by six-year-old Paul, who from February to June began every piece of writing with 'I like . . .'. During this time Paul liked, 'when I went to the beach . . . Clifford the big red dog . . . the caterpillar . . . caterpillars . . . the rain . . . when I went swimming' and much else. Many of the items which he 'liked' were also repeated, often being spelled differently on a number of occasions. For example 'beach' began 'doecht', then became 'beac', and finally 'beach'.

Repetition of theme

Seven-year-old Simon repeated the same theme for several weeks. First he wrote about racing cars, then he moved to other pieces about racing—the boat race, the running race, rockets racing—and then back to the car races.

Eleven-year-old Andrew wrote science fiction. Each piece had different characters and settings, but basically followed the same plot and solution. He also read within this theme.

Another form of repetition which occurs with older children is the 'bush fire' topic. This is a topic begun by one child which then races through the class like a bush fire. There may be several variations on it but it remains the basic topic. In a Year 3 class it was the 'Fruit People', based on the Mr Men series. There was Miss Banana, Mr Apple, Miss Plum, etc. In a Year 5 class it was 'Monster'. There was 'The Green Monster', 'The Monster without a Head', 'The Monster Who Ate Children' and so on.

Reading the same author is another form of repetition found in older classrooms. With younger children it tends to be reading the same book over and over again.

It is difficult to be conclusive about the function of this strategy. Perhaps the child is simply enjoying writing about the same topic or reading the same book. Perhaps it serves as a kind of safety net above which the learner can try out new hypotheses and/or explore new relationships—a kind of framework within which to experiment or take risks without any real fear or danger of failing. The teacher or a peer has given some positive feedback to the type of writing the child is doing and the child feels comfortable or safe.

All learners tend to follow this pattern. We like to consolidate and practise what we know we can do before branching out into something new. Consider the champion high board diver in this light.

We also found a difference in the degree of repetition between ESB and NESB children. The NESB children's frequency of repetition tends to be higher and persists for longer periods of time. Thus Ivanka's continual inclusion of 'house with TV aerial', 'sun' and 'flowers' in her drawing with the accompanying random set of letters was labelled 'prolonged' repetition. Eventually, when Ivanka's growth in English had reached a sufficient level, she began to include new items in her drawings and in her tellings of them.

It should be kept in mind that these repetitions are typically voluntary in the sense that of all the options available, given the freedom they have in their learning setting, these children choose to repeat. This is different from doing repeated sets of exercises which are imposed by the teacher, and for which there is no choice. But given the freedom, the expectations, and the other features of the context, repetition is a common coping strategy. We can describe it as:

Coping by choosing to repeat previously successful or partially successful forms of behaviour.

Assistance from/interaction with peers

A common strategy initiated by children was to seek and receive assistance from their peers. This assistance took two distinct forms.

As a consequence of a direct request for help

This occurred when a child directly requested help of anyone who was listening or from a specific child.

Setting: a Kindergarten classroom

SARAH: Shelley, how do you spell 'sky'?
SHELLEY: S-E-Y.
SARAH: No. S-C-E-Y.
SHELLEY: No, S-C-E-Y-E.
ROSS: My sister wrote that word and it's got 'K' in it.
SARAH: S-K-Y-E.
SHELLEY: No, S-K-E-Y.
ROSS: I think it's S-K-Y.

Setting: a Kindergarten classroom

HANADI: How do you write 'witch'?
WASSIM: Here, it's here. (*He goes over to a box of cards and takes out a card with a picture of a witch and the letter 'w' and word 'witch' written on it.*) There (*pointing to the word 'witch'*). That's 'witch'.

Setting: a Year 3 classroom

SCOTT: Paul, does this sound right? (*Scott pushes his piece of writing in front of Paul.*)
PAUL: No . . . Did you go on the waterslide once or more times than that?
SCOTT: I went on it two times and then the last time the big kids pushed in front of me, so I didn't get my go.
PAUL: Well, you have to say 'you went on the waterslide two times before the big kids pushed in.'

In classrooms where children can speak to other children in a first language other than English, this type of assistance also occurs. Unfortunately most of us are unaware of what the children are asking each other. The following is an interpretation of what was said between two Greek students in Year 5, and demonstrates the value of NESB children using their first language when they need to.

Setting: a Year 5 classroom

ROULLA: Sonia, how do you say in English 'not happy' (*said in English*)?
SONIA: 'Not happy'—you mean 'sad'?
ROULLA: No, there is a word with 'happy' in it that means 'not happy' (*again 'not happy' is said in English*).
SONIA: (*after some discussion about the meaning of 'sad'*) I know. (*In English*) un-happy, un-happy.

As a consequence of incidental exposure to information about the conventions of writing through spontaneous interaction with other children

A Kindergarten setting

SARAH: I am, I am, I yam, yam, yam (*laughter*).

RYAN: Yam, yam, yam. Huh, Sarah. Yam ends in 'am'.

SARAH: And it starts with 'Yuh'.

RYAN: How do you write a 'Yuh'?

SARAH: It's in your name (*pointing to his name tag*). Look. R-Yuh-A-N (*letters R, A, N are named, but Y is sounded*).

RYAN: No, that's a Y (*letter name used*).

SARAH: It's a 'Yuh' too.

RYAN: I never knew that before.

Setting: a Year 2 classroom

HAROLD: How do you write their?

STANLEY: Which their do you mean?

SUZANNE: There is only one their.

STANLEY: No, there are two ways of writing their: 't-h-i-r' and 't-h-e-r-e'. (*Harold has gone on with his writing, ignoring this continuing conversation.*)

SUZANNE: Here, write them; show me.

STANLEY: (*writing 'thir', 'there' on the corner of his paper*) There—see? (*Pointing to each word*) their, there.

SUZANNE: That's not how you write 'their' (*pointing to 'thir'. She takes her pencil and adds the 'e'*).

STANLEY: Oh yeah. Their. 'This is their dog.' And this there goes 'There is the dog.'

SUZANNE: There are lots of words that are spelt differently but say the same, aren't there? (*And the two continue to find more sets of words like this.*)

In classrooms in which we have observed this strategy at work there must be a certain amount of talk allowed by the teacher. Teachers trust that the children's talk is to do with their writing. It is also important that NESB children know that they can speak to each other in their first language. Teachers support children in the use of this strategy by suggesting to them 'Go and ask . . .'. But it is also a consequence of the setting: children with a common task, seated in such a way that they are close enough to interact and talk and given the freedom to do just that, will make the best of the situation and draw on the knowledge and information of their peers.

Put learners together in this kind of situation, and the way they share the different kinds of knowledge that each brings to the task becomes obvious. Such interaction is at the core of most learning. In the older classrooms we found that it is the major underlying strategy, as it is built

Children enjoy the responsibility of helping each other with their writing.

into the whole rationale of the classroom structure. It underlies the activities designed by the teacher and the way time is distributed. The children are explicitly encouraged and expected to interact with and assist each other. It is often referred to as 'peer tutoring', and can be described as:

Coping by using the peer resources immediately available, either by direct request or through interaction commenced for another reason.

Assistance from/interaction with the teacher

This strategy refers to the seeking of assistance from the teacher or any other adult in the room. It is sought either by a direct request for help:

SHAUN: Miss B—how do you write 'vasectomy'? My dad had a vasectomy

or by initiating an interaction:

LAM: I read now? I read now?

It has been our experience that ESB children make many more direct requests for assistance when they come up against a problem or difficulty than do NESB children, who are more likely to bring their finished product to the teacher for comment and interaction (and approval). Why this occurs is unclear. It may be that as long as NESB children are unsure of what is expected of them in the writing context because of their limitation in English, they need the type of feedback from the teacher which tells them they are doing the 'right thing'. ESB children, on the other hand, are confident English users and know both when they need some assistance and how to ask for it at the point of need. As NESB children become more proficient in their English the difference between the two groups diminishes.

Essentially this strategy is a double-edged one in the sense that teachers also use it to keep track of their children—to monitor, assess and evaluate. With older children it seems to be mainly teacher-initiated. Children only come to the teacher as a last resort, and so the teacher often will initiate interaction as she or he moves around the classroom. It appears to be a common strategy which we can call:

Coping by asking/seeking information from the teacher.

The use of temporary spelling

There have been many well-researched and documented studies in recent years on the use of 'temporary'[1] or functional spelling by young children: for instance, Read (1974), Bissex (1980), Ferreiro & Teberosky (1982) and Bouffler (1984). These studies demonstrate conclusively that when young learners are given opportunity and encouragement to create written texts, they will attempt to create meaning using unconventional spellings (temporary spelling). They also suggest that as these children continue to write using their temporary or invented spellings, they gradually proceed through a series of approximations to the conventional forms of spelling, experimenting with different unconventional versions of the same word. Simon's attempts to write 'saw' over a six-month period proceeded from 's' to 'sor', 'swa', and finally 'saw'.

Bouffler's work (1984, pp.56–57) has been valuable in identifying and describing a range of strategies which young writers typically employ while engaged in such writing.

---

[1]Many teachers refer to these spellings as 'invented' spellings. We prefer to describe them as 'temporary' spellings for two reasons:
i) the notion of 'invention' carries negative connotations for many teachers and parents, and
ii) 'temporary' describes them more realistically and makes them analogous to baby-talk.

1. Spelling as it sounds
This refers to what is generally known as phonetic spelling and is based on the assumption of a direct sound/symbol relationship: e.g. STASHON-station; SISERS-scissors.

2. Spelling as it sounds out
This strategy was identified being used by children but was not seen used by adults. It involves the exaggeration of sound, so that phonetic features not normally represented are heard and represented: e.g. HUW-who; HAFH-half.

3. Spelling as it articulates
This strategy makes use of the articulatory aspects of sound, particularly place of articulation. Sounds are represented on the basis of where they are made: e.g. BRIF-brief; CHRIDAGEN-tried again.

4. Spelling as it means
This strategy represents semantic rather than phonological units. It underlies much standard spelling: e.g. sign-signal; nation-nationality. Non-standard example: WASUPONATIM-Once upon a time.

5. Spelling as it looks
All spelling involves this strategy to some extent. As its name suggests, it uses graphic patterning, or visual memory: e.g. OEN-one; SHCOOL-school; NIGT-night.

6. Spelling by analogy
This strategy is based on the principle that what has been learned in one situation can be applied to another: e.g. REALISTICK-realistic; RESKYOU-rescue.

7. Spelling by linguistic context
The spelling of a word may be affected by the linguistic environment in which it occurs. It is not altogether surprising to find 'any' written immediately under the word 'envelope' as 'eny'.

8. Spelling by reference to authority
The authority may be other children, adults, or other writers (i.e. other written books or material). When other books, such as the dictionary, are used, we must employ all or some of the other strategies to find the word we are trying to write.

9. Opting for an alternate surface structure
If we do not know how to spell a word, we use a word we know we can spell.

10. Placing the onus on the reader
This strategy is used when text is handwritten. The writer makes the spelling indeterminate and leaves it to the reader to decide whether, for example, it is 'ie' or 'ei'.

One or several of these strategies may be involved in any one spelling produced. They seldom, if ever, exist in isolation but rather in transaction with each other and with other aspects of the writing process. It is difficult in the face of such complexity to continue to insist that spelling is a single skill.

The children we have observed confirm the evidence from earlier studies. They too used temporary spellings; they employed one, some or all of the strategies identified by Read (1974), Bissex (1980), Ferreiro & Teberosky (1982) and Bouffler (1984): they refined their approximations over time and they experimented with different functional variations of the same word.

There were some other findings, however, which need to be discussed in the light of the classroom observations we have made.

Reluctance to 'have a go' at unknown words

Both ESB and NESB children were reluctant during the first month of schooling to approximate, to use temporary spelling. They seemed to prefer to operate within a kind of safety framework by copying from the environmental print, or by using rote-memorised conventional spellings. They would happily draw and talk about their drawing, but they were reluctant to write about their theme using temporary spellings.

The notion that approximating was an acceptable strategy to use when creating text did not appear to take hold with the majority of children until approximately one month into the school year. In some classrooms the teachers decided to demonstrate the various strategies which could be used to 'have a go' at writing an unknown word.

For instance, in one classroom the teacher would write a draft of the class daily News on the board before writing the conventional form into the Newsbook. When writing in front of the children she would 'think aloud', asking questions such as: 'How does "going" start? Go-ing; g-o-ing; g-. That's what I need. Now how do you write a "g"?' When children offered to help she would gladly accept their assistance, often passing the chalk to them to write the letter or word. The draft on the board looked like:

KP r go o u pcnc.

This was written later into the Newsbook in conventional form:

KP are going on a picnic.

These demonstrations served not only to show children various strategies they could use to approximate spelling but also that their teacher was willing to accept the temporary forms and that she expected them to 'have a go' at doing the same. She also demonstrated that temporary spellings really are temporary—she erased them from the chalkboard when they were no longer needed. Furthermore, she demonstrated that 'public' writing needs to be conventional so that we can all read it.

In a few cases, however, this reluctance was a little more difficult to overcome, and after further investigation it was traced to a mixture of family, social class and cultural factors. Within the group of ESB children those most reluctant to approximate had been influenced by parents (usually from middle-class professional backgrounds) who conveyed to their children expectations of correctness and error avoidance.

Within the NESB group, the South-East Asian children were, on the whole, the most reluctant to approximate. Teachers believed this was due to both cultural and social influences. After further discussion with members of the Vietnamese, Chinese and Korean communities, it was found that generally these cultures encourage error avoidance as a valued trait, especially with regard to education. Older brothers and sisters also seem to give their younger siblings the expectation that they should write 'error-free'. Attempts at approximating words are, it seems, sometimes ridiculed by the older siblings.

Some children begin to approximate their spellings and then quite suddenly refuse. Six-year-old Ryan, for example, had been producing pages of writing. He sounded each word out audibly as he wrote it. This willingness to approximate abruptly stopped. He would only write words for which he knew the conventional spelling or which he could find in the room. When he attempted to write he constantly asked the teacher for the 'right way' to spell words. What had happened was that he'd begun to read and was aware that his spellings were not conventional. 'I just write lots of mistakes and those other writers [meaning the authors of the books he was reading] don't make all the mistakes.'

The teacher spent a great deal of time explaining to Ryan and the rest of the class that authors also have to draft their writing and make mistakes, but the editor 'fixes them up' before the books are published for children to read. A compromise was set up with Ryan: if he wrote the first sound and any other sounds or letters he could hear or 'see in his head', the teacher would add the rest for him.

Given time and a strong expectation from the teacher that approximating spellings was acceptable practice, all children we've observed eventually began to 'have a go', even the South-East Asian children.

Most common spelling strategy used by ESB children

By the end of the second month of schooling, the majority of ESB children were using many of the spelling strategies which Bouffler has described. However, 'sounding-out' (phonemic segmentation) quickly became predominant. As their reading developed they began to use 'spelling as it looks' as well, though they often confused the letter groupings and placed them in the wrong order. For instance, in one piece six-year-old Simon wrote:

oen-one; swa-saw; rase-race; cold-could; niht-night.

Most common spelling strategy used by NESB children

The NESB children, many of whom came to school with little or no English, were slow to 'have a go' at spellings using phonemic segmentation. Cambourne (1986, p.136) has argued that 'the ability to segment language is a function of the degree of control that one has over language.' The most common spelling strategy among NESB children was using letters which bore no phonemic relationship to the intended word, to place-hold meaning. These children relied on the environmental print.

In some cases a different set of letters would be used to represent the same concept, but generally there was some evidence of a kind of 'visual consistency' developing over time. This visual consistency took two forms.

1. Using different letters, but keeping the number used constant (or nearly constant) across words, e.g:
    Time 1 SAZSL — caterpillar (5 letters)
    Time 2 MRTLS — caterpillar (5 letters)
    Time 3 SMZL — caterpillar (4 letters).

2. Using the same group of letters (or nearly the same group of letters) to represent the same concept, e.g:
    FZV, FVZ, ZVF used to represent 'flower' on a number of occasions.

What we can see happening with young children as they come to grips with English spellings seems to be dependent on their confidence and competence in using the language of the classroom: Standard English. In particular, children from other cultural and linguistic backgrounds bring to school differing levels of knowledge and understanding about the written form of English, and so their use of the various coping strategies will differ in manner and frequency too. Teachers also need to be aware that although these child-oriented, child-developed and child-controlled coping strategies are temporary scaffolds, they are highly functional in the written language learning of the child.

CHAPTER THREE

Gathering the Threads

Classrooms identified as 'process-writing' or 'process-oriented' class-rooms demonstrate similar conditions operating in them. Within the learning settings these conditions (listed on p.7) operate in such a way that they orchestrate the development of certain types of learning behaviours, which emerge as children attempt to solve the written language puzzle. We have referred to such learning behaviours as 'coping strategies'—strategies which children develop and control for themselves as they grapple with that part of the written language puzzle they are attempting to learn at that particular moment. We've also argued that these strategies are a form of scaffolding, in the sense that children erect them as temporary structures to support themselves in their learning. As learning occurs the scaffolds are removed by the children, and others serving a different function may be erected.

Not only are these coping strategies predictable—they are highly functional because they constantly provide those who belong to such classrooms access to three different kinds of opportunities necessary for solving the written language puzzle. These are opportunities for:

- gleaning information about written language which can be used to tease out the precise relationships between reading, writing and language through:
    - —lots of opportunity to use it, to play with it
    - —demonstrations of how written language works
- formulating and testing hypotheses concerning this information through:
    - —providing ways to try out, talk about, share, approximate written language

- gaining feedback necessary for confirming, modifying, or rejecting any hypothesis from:
  —demonstrations
  —opportunities to share, talk, seek assistance from peers and teachers about written language.

Each one of the coping strategies described earlier contributes to access to these three kinds of opportunities in different ways and to different degrees. For example, the information necessary for teasing out the relationships which exist between reading, writing and language can be gleaned from any one, or from a combination of the coping strategies. Learners can use environmental print, engage in repetition, seek or receive assistance from peers or teachers and use temporary spellings in their quest to sort out how print works. They similarly use the strategies to formulate and/or test hypotheses, and then to gain the necessary feedback to confirm, reject or modify their hypotheses about the written language puzzle.

Although the speed with which ESB and NESB children solve the puzzle differs, the basic process underlying the learning which occurs is essentially the same for each group, viz. one of hypothesis testing. This testing is performed by using the coping strategies, which children bring to bear on their learning in order to meet the expectations and conditions which exist in the learning settings set up by their teachers. In other words, the social setting orchestrates certain kinds of behaviours which increase the probability that learning about the written form of language will take place.

If we synthesise the thinking of researchers like Graves (in Walshe 1981) and Dyson (1982), and writers like Smith (1981), and we add this to what emerged from our research, a succinct descriptive overview of the processes involved in such learning can be presented, as on the page opposite.

How does it all work?

The relationship between the social setting and coping behaviours of the children is consistent with many theories stemming from many branches of linguistics and psychology. Basically these theories assert that settings exert an influence on the way people behave and use language when they choose to participate in them (or find themselves in them) and that there are particular settings with clearly defined characteristics within which behaviour and language can be predicted with a great deal of accuracy.

Thus, settings known as 'supermarkets' exert certain pressures on those who enter them. These pressures constrain shoppers to behave in certain ways which are highly predictable. People in supermarkets move at a certain speed, stopping every now and then to remove something from the shelves and put it in their trolleys. Their language is

The Written Language Puzzle — How Do Children Solve It?

Majority of children arrive at kindergarten with a vague, general understanding that reading, writing and language are related in some way.

↓

In order to solve the written language puzzle they

↓

need to understand the *precise* connection between reading, writing and language—including:
• writers' intentions are expressed through specifically arranged symbols
• symbols are related in arbitrary but precise ways to formal characteristics of speech
• readers can only perceive messages when encoded in such specific ways.

↓

They develop coping strategies which enable the following to occur.

↓

They select, interpret, integrate information from reading/writing language models/demonstrations around them.	i.e. →	'In attempting to create a message children must organize and put into action their conceptions of writing.'
↓		↓
They make hypotheses about relationships.	i.e. →	'In attempting to read or have others read their writing they must face the inevitable contradictions between what they thought they were doing and what in fact they did.'
↓		
They test hypotheses.		
↓		
Hypotheses do not work out.		↓
↓		
Puzzlement results.	i.e. →	'On-going activities get suspended—learner becomes tense, aroused; a variety of attentional, curiosity, exploratory, and other information-seeking behaviours ensue . . . . Reflection leads to refinement.' (Dyson 1982, p.833)
↓		
Hypotheses refined.		

typically associated with the task in hand. The setting has, among other things, a certain physical structure which almost forces those who enter to move in certain directions towards certain predetermined ends. It also has certain themes and processes which people talk about, engage in, read and so on.

Similarly the settings known as 'church' suggest certain predictable behaviours, including standing, sitting, kneeling, singing, responding, listening to the preacher, and so on. Other behaviours, such as swearing, running up and down the aisles, or playing football over the pews, would seem inappropriate. And we need to learn the 'rules' of behaviour and the language use of such settings, so that we know when to kneel, when to sing and why we should not play football over the pews. In order to do this we use coping strategies. For instance, if we find ourselves in a 'church' setting which differs from the kind we know and find predictable—say a mosque—we develop coping strategies to allow us to behave appropriately and use the language of that not so predictable setting. We might take more time to move from one position to another so that we can watch others to see what position we should move to; we might 'mouth' words so that others will think we know what we are saying. Eventually, if we spend a long enough time in that new setting, we will learn the behaviours, expectations and language used, and the setting will become predictable.

The settings which have been labelled 'process-oriented' classrooms are similar in this respect. As behaviour settings they have a certain unique structure which is an amalgam of the furniture, the books, charts and materials, the language used, the expectations of the individuals who maintain them, the rituals or 'rules of operation' which have to be adhered to, and so on. It is also apparent that these classroom settings orchestrate behaviours and language which are synomorphic with (i.e. have a good 'fit' with) what we know about the kind of learning which takes place in more naturally occurring settings, particularly the learning-to-talk setting. And the fact that the same patterns of behaviour have been observed in many different classrooms over an extended period of time strongly suggests that there is some functional, predictable relationship between the setting and the kinds of behaviours and language use which occur within it.

The implications for this kind of predictable relationship are interesting. The first is that if teachers can organise their classrooms so that the conditions described on p. 7 are all strongly present, then the learners in those classrooms ought to behave in predictable ways; i.e. the coping strategies described should begin to emerge as the children take on responsibility to solve the written language puzzle. Furthermore, as these strategies do begin to emerge, the evidence is that their use is functional and inevitably leads the learner-writer to make significant gains in the resolution of the written language puzzle which he/she is trying to solve.

Secondly, the relationship provides a framework for observing, comparing and evaluating different children's responses to the process-oriented context. For instance, are some using only a narrow set of coping strategies? Why? Should some children be advised to try other strategies?

Thirdly, it may be possible to ascertain how any one, or any specific combination of the conditions described on p.7 relate to the incidence and balance of coping strategies which ultimately emerge in any classroom. It would be valuable to know, for example, how the nature and/or quality of the print units available to learners affect the degree to which the 'environmental print' coping strategy is used, and so on. It would also be of interest to tease out how various phases of the hypothesis-formulation/hypothesis-modification cycle relate to the various kinds of coping strategies used by different learners.

However, the most obvious implication of all this is disturbing in its simplicity, for it suggests a series of links that go something like this.

Establish the classroom conditions (which lead to children to use)

↓

a set of coping strategies (which lead to children to)

↓

learning about the relationships/concepts/knowledge necessary to operate the written form of the language.

In one sense the simplicity is obvious: the conditions described on p.7 are analogous to those which operate when children learn to talk. On the surface, learning to talk the language of the culture into which one has been born is one of the 'simplest' achievements known to the human race; it's usually painless, almost unconsciously done, nearly always successful, and seems to 'just occur' when the conditions for learning have been established. Once they are established, young learner-talkers develop certain coping strategies which, when employed, inevitably produce competent (within that culture) language users.

At a more macroscopic level this simplicity is, of course, illusory. It conceals a complexity of interacting and transacting factors which are excruciatingly complicated and detailed. However, though complex and intricate, the process is surprisingly robust and predictable. So it is with these process-oriented classrooms—despite the incredibly complex and intricate relationships which are part of them, they are also very robust and very predictable.

Thus, rather than these classrooms being described as 'chaotic', or 'confused', or 'unstructured', it can be argued that they are orderly,

Trung's classroom allows him the freedom to choose his own strategies to solve the written language puzzle.

theoretically predictable settings, in which behaviour is governed by certain principles which have been theoretically derived. The theory predicts that once the setting has been established, and all the factors which make it *that* particular setting are set in motion, then behaviour and learning will proceed in certain predictable ways, allowing children to choose the coping strategy which best suits the language learning they are coming to grips with at that point in time.

The problem, of course, lies in convincing those like the disenchanted infants teacher described at the beginning of this book, that these relationships do exist, and that robust, powerful learning results.

CHAPTER FOUR

How the Theory Looks in Practice

What has been discussed in the previous chapters is an explanation of the ways in which children learn 'how to mean in print' within classroom settings that aim to be as 'natural' as the settings in which children learn how to mean in the spoken form of language—listening and talking.

In this chapter we want to demonstrate how this looks in the writing of two children. But, before doing so, it is important to discuss the relationship between the so-called 'language arts': talking, listening, reading and writing. Although teachers often deal with talking, listening, reading and writing as separate components of language, this separation in effect is quite artificial. To facilitate the learning environment in the classroom teachers need to understand the strong relationships between the four language components.

Carolyn Burke has tried to capture the essential notions of this thinking in a visual metaphor entitled 'The Linguistic Data Pool'. She suggests that each of us can be considered to have a personal pool of language knowledge or data which is constantly being added to by the language encounters we experience. The data for the pool enters as a result of us being involved in talking, listening, reading and writing experiences. We in turn draw on this pool of data when we are involved in talking, listening, reading and writing experiences. The central notions Burke attempts to portray are:

1. What language users learn from a language encounter feeds a common pool of linguistic data which can be drawn upon in a subsequent language encounter.

2. Oral language encounters provide data for written language encounters and vice versa.

3. Growth in a given expression of language must be seen as a
   multilingual event; in reading, for example, hearing a set of directions read, encountering written language with others, listening to
   a book, talking about a newspaper article, or attempting to write
   one's own story, all support growth and development in literacy.

   　　　　　　　　　　　　　　(Harste, Woodward & Burke 1984, p.210)

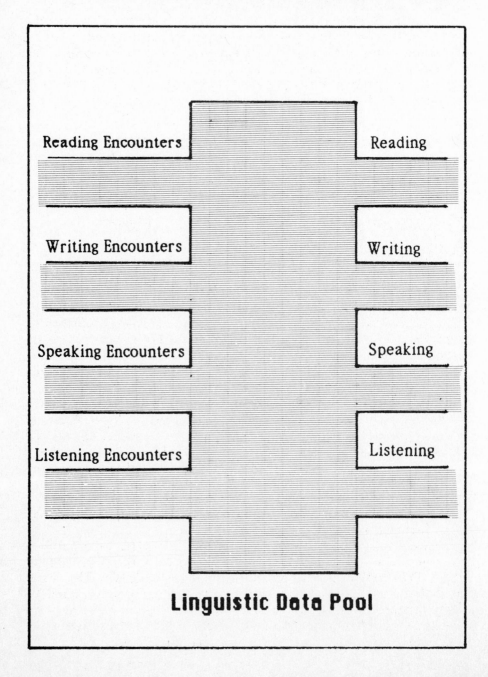

Linguistic Data Pool

An important outcome of this thinking is that it proposes a parallel development for the 'language arts'; that the cognitive processes involved in composing meaning from (listening, reading) and through (talking, writing) language are similar, but realised in different ways.

Children enter their first year of school with their own personal linguistic data pool which has grown out of the social interactions of their culture and has served them well until this point. For many of the children entering our schools, however, this means that although they have a language that has fulfilled the language purposes within their culture, they come to school with little or no knowledge of the 'language of the classroom—Standard English'. Teachers need to establish an educational setting which allows children to draw on their personal linguistic data pool and at the same time to add various 'new' language experiences to that pool.

The story of two children's writing development

The following two case studies show how children may enter school with vastly differing linguistic and cultural backgrounds. In what way does this affect their personal linguistic data pool?

Sarah entered school at the age of 5 years 2 months. She came from an English-speaking background. Her parents were both employed in professional positions. Sarah would have had many encounters with talking, listening, reading and writing in English. Her personal linguistic data pool and the language of the classroom were closely aligned.

Lam entered school at the age of 4 years 10 months. Lam came from a Vietnamese-speaking background, arriving in Australia with his family when he was eighteen months old. Both his parents were unemployed and spoke very little English. Lam's personal linguistic data pool was Vietnamese, quite different from the language of the classroom.

Although these children attended different schools, they both spent their first year of school in a setting that could be called 'process-oriented', i.e. the conditions exemplified earlier in this book were clearly identifiable.

What the following examples of writing show is that both children attempted to solve the written language puzzle in their first year of school. They both used various coping strategies to do that. The rate at which they accomplished this task, the choice of coping strategy and the length of time each strategy was used were contingent upon how each child's personal linguistic data pool aligned with the language of the classroom.

LAM'S WRITING *(case study researched by Jan Turbill)*

Sample 1: March

Background

Lam had been at school for three weeks. He knew very little English. But there were three other Vietnamese-speaking children in the class and during 'writing time' they sat together, chatting in Vietnamese as they drew their pictures. 'Goldilocks and the Three Bears' was the central focus of the class setting. The teacher had told the children the story several times with much miming and dramatisation. She had read the story to them from a book and they had been learning the rhyme, 'When Goldilocks went to the house of the bears'.

SARAH'S WRITING (*case study researched by Brian Cambourne*)

Sample 1: February 4th

Background
On the first day of school Sarah and her classmates were given paper and pencils and asked to 'write as much as you can'.

Descriptive Account of the Process
Sarah wrote 'cat', 'mat', 'sat' down the left-hand side of the page. When asked if she could write any more, she began the second column, announcing to no-one in particular, 'I'll do "at" words.' She worked quickly on her 'at story' as if this sequence was a well-practised one

Descriptive Account of the Process

Lam began drawing the house, then added the 'house for cars' on the side. He drew 'three flower', 'sun', 'moon' and 'some grass'. When he was telling his teacher about his drawing he couldn't think of the English word for 'moon', so he spoke in his first language to the other children.

His teacher prompted with, 'Is it a banana?'

'No,' grinned Lam. 'Not banana . . . moon, yea, moon.'

Then, touching each item again, he said. 'House, car house, three flower, some grass, sun. MOON.'

Comments

This was the first of many pieces which included a house, flowers, grass, sun and moon. Lam is using two coping strategies: using a related activity and repetition. He can talk about these items in English with success and feels safe with them. He feels he is achieving the expectations of the writing setting. His teacher comes and listens to him talk about his piece and praises him for his attempts. The drawings are serving as a basis for his oral language development and the teacher is constantly helping Lam to extend his English. It would seem obvious that he needs a minimal degree of control of English before he will be able to write it.

COPING STRATEGIES BEING USED	LANGUAGE LEARNING TAKING PLACE
• Using related activity—drawing. • Repetition—repeats picture items.	• Developing oral language in English. • Drawing in 'writing' allows Lam to talk about what he knows in English.

which had been internalised. Sarah could read it all back on request. She did the drawing after the writing. This she called a pattern.

Comments

After this writing episode Sarah was interviewed about her writing. Among other things she was asked the following questions:

TEACHER: Are you a good writer?

SARAH: Yes.

TEACHER: Why?

SARAH: 'Cause I get all my words right and it's neat.

TEACHER: Do you like writing?

SARAH: Yes.

TEACHER: Why?

SARAH: 'Cause I'm good at it.

TEACHER: Who taught you to write?

SARAH: Mummy. (*Sarah's mother is a teacher.*)

Sarah has, she thinks, solved the written language puzzle. Good writing to her is 'getting words right' and being 'neat'. Good writing also goes down the page from top to bottom, with the words forming vertical columns. These are obviously hypotheses about writing she has tested before coming to school, and she has had them confirmed (perhaps not intentionally) by the adults or older siblings who were helping her.

COPING STRATEGIES BEING USED	LANGUAGE LEARNING TAKING PLACE
• Repetition of known words learnt at home.	• Writing *is* words. A good writer is neat and correct.

Sample 2: April

Background
Writing time was now a predictable part of the daily routine, occurring from 10.15 to 10.45am. Each session began with a sharing time in which the teacher might read to the children or show and discuss some child's writing. On this day she had asked the children to 'do some writing like I do' and had then demonstrated some writing on the chalkboard. She wrote the class news: 'Tomorrow K2 is going to the zoo'. As she wrote, she sounded words out aloud and asked herself questions like: 'What does that word start with? Where is that word written in the room?' She encouraged the children to join in and help her and at times gave the chalk to a child to write a letter or word.

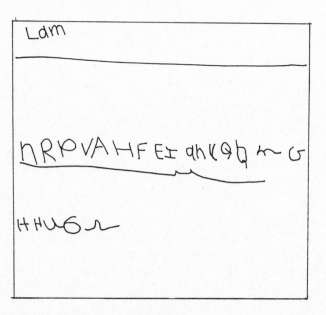

Descriptive Account of the Process
Lam took his paper and wrote his name up in the top left-hand corner from memory. He then drew a line across the page underneath his name. He wrote a series of letters, often looking up at charts on the wall or other children's name cards to copy the letters. The last five 'shapes' he wrote very quickly without appearing to refer to anything in the room. He then drew a line under these 'letters'.

His teacher came to him and said: 'Good boy, Lam. You have written a lot. Will you tell me what your writing says?'

Lam traced his finger along the line of letters from left to right. When he came to the end of the row he simply returned to the beginning and traced his finger along the row again. He repeated this action several times until he had finished telling the story that went with the 'writing'.

Sample 2: February 11th

Background

Writing time had become a regular daily session. The teacher had made folders and the children had decorated them. They knew that at the end of writing time they were to put their piece into the folder. The teacher began each writing session by reading to the children, or by writing in front of them and then simply announcing, 'It's writing time'. She then moved around the room writing the date on each piece and talking to as many children as possible about their writing. This particular morning she had asked the children to help her read the labels around the room: e.g. 'I'm the toilet door. I'm a sad dog. I'm a happy boy. This is the teacher's chair.'

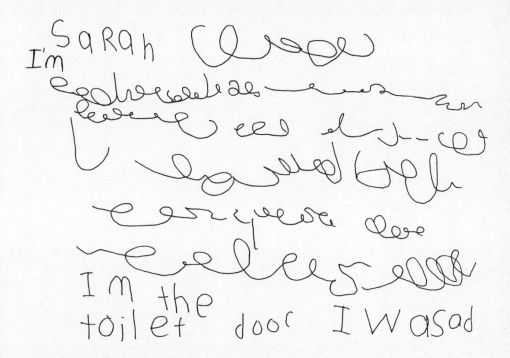

Descriptive Account of the Process

Sarah wrote her name in the middle-top-left section of her paper. She then copied 'I'm' from the environmental print, 'I'm the table'. She went on to write from left to right in 'lines' in what appeared to be an imitation of adult cursive. When asked what she was doing, she replied: 'Grown-up writing.'

TEACHER:	What does it say?
SARAH:	I can't read grown-up writing, I can only write it.
TEACHER:	Can you write any more?
SARAH:	I'll do some other writing.

'When Goldilocks went to the house of the bears, she see porridge. She try Father Bear porridge. Too hot. She try Mother Bear porridge. Too cold. She try Baby Bear. She eat it ALL up.'

'That's wonderful Lam,' said his teacher.

Lam picked up his pencil and wrote some more 'letters'. He began to 'read' them, tracing his finger along the row.

'Grandma TOO sick and Red Riding Hood . . .' (he stopped and touched the shape that looked like a '6'). 'Look! A number 6.'

Comments

Lam has begun to use a new coping strategy: using environmental print. He has responded to the teacher's request to 'write like I do'. There are times when Lam makes up letters, which we believe is similar to drawing and is thus the coping strategy: using a related activity. He is demonstrating that he knows that 'reading' in English goes from left to right, and he draws on his growing personal linguistic pool to tell the story of his 'writing'. He actually uses the language of the rhyme and then the story he has heard over and over again some weeks earlier: 'When Goldilocks went to the house of the bears. . . She try Father Bear porridge. Too hot.'

When he decides to do some more 'writing', he begins to tell another story he had heard over and over, 'Red Riding Hood'. Interestingly, he recognises a symbol in his own writing when he notices the shape that looks like a 6.

COPING STRATEGIES BEING USED	LANGUAGE LEARNING TAKING PLACE
• Using environmental print—copying random letters and placing meaning on them. • Using related activity—making up (drawing) letters.	• Writing can tell a story. • Written language moves from left to right.

Sample 3: May

Background

Lam's competence in English was increasing. He tended to act as interpreter for the other three Vietnamese children. He could also tell the teacher in English the gist of what the group had been talking about in Vietnamese. The class focus was now 'The Gingerbread Boy'.

Descriptive Account of the Process

Lam had drawn the large house and police car and the spidery object in the top right-hand corner. His teacher came and sat beside him, but before she spoke to him another child approached her and 'read' her

She began copying from the labels around the room. She wrote: 'Im the toilet door' and 'Iwasad' from 'I'm a sad dog'. She read these pointing to the words as she read.

Comments

Since her first attempts at writing the week before Sarah seems to have realised that she hasn't completely resolved the written language puzzle. During the week the teacher had demonstrated writing in front of the children on the overhead projector, using her own cursive style. Sarah had felt the need to try out this 'new' hypothesis. When it didn't work, in the sense that it didn't mean anything to her or the teacher, she reverted to something she knew she could make meaning with. Sarah is making use of the coping strategy: copying environmental print. She is also falling back onto a coping strategy she knows has worked in the past—repeating a 'successful' strategy. She selects print that she can read and is therefore meaningful to her.

COPING STRATEGIES BEING USED	LANGUAGE LEARNING TAKING PLACE
• Copying labels from the environment which she can read. • Using related activity—making up 'grown-up' writing.	• Writing goes from left to right and from top to bottom. • Writing is to be read. • Made-up writing can't be read and thus has no meaning.

Sample 3: February 24th

Background

The class routine during writing was becoming quite established, with children chattering to each other about their work and also other experiences. The teacher had been talking to the children about crossing the road and had drawn a set of traffic lights on the chalkboard.

Descriptive Account of the Process

Sarah wrote her name and announced: 'I'll do some "at" words.' She wrote 'The cat in The hat' down the page, one word under the other, obviously from memory. She then announced to the other children on

writing. Sonia had written 'Iwtmh'—'I went to my house.' The teacher praised Sonia's writing attempts and showed Lam and the other children at his group of tables. Lam picked up his pencil and at the top of the page began to write a random set of letters which he appeared to be writing from memory. These he 'read' to his teacher, tracing his finger from left to right and back again along the row until the story was complete.

'This is a apartment house. Someone in the house is fighting and someone get a gun and kill him and him die and the police come and Spiderman.'

Comments

Lam is no longer repeating the same picture items although he still uses drawing as a related activity for writing. When the teacher showed (i.e. demonstrated) Sonia's writing to Lam, he reacted to that demonstration and expectation and he also began to 'write'. He uses the coping strategy of random copying of letters to achieve this purpose. Although Lam cannot recognise any of these letters, he uses them as place-holders for the meaning he wants to express. When 'reading' his writing he does tell a story. Quite possibly if he were asked to 'read' the letters on the next day, he would 'read' a slightly different story.

COPING STRATEGIES BEING USED	LANGUAGE LEARNING TAKING PLACE
• Using related activity—drawing. • Copying random letters and placing meaning on them.	• Oral English language developing. • Writing can tell a story—using 'book language'.

her table that she had seen the film 'E.T.'. She wrote 'Et' under 'hat', then said: 'I'll do some more "at" words', and wrote 'cat, at, The, hat'. She then started a new column and began to copy from an environmental label, 'I'm the doll's house'. She wrote 'Im' and 'The' after only one look at the label. But to write 'dolls' she needed to look up at the word four times. She seemed to forget 'house'. She then began to draw (copy) the traffic lights on the board. Sarah read all her writing to the teacher. When reading 'I'm the doll's . . .', she realised she had left out 'house' but did not attempt to write it.

Comments
Sarah appears to be consolidating what she knows about writing. She is using the coping strategies of repetition (by writing the 'at' words, in column) and of using environmental print, writing it also in columns. This latter use of columns is unusual because none of the labels in the room are written in columns. Sarah seems to be taking responsibility for what she will attend to and learn, and what she will ignore. She has apparently chosen to ignore the demonstrations in the room of left-to-right setting out, repeating what she has successfully used before—columns.

COPING STRATEGIES BEING USED	LANGUAGE LEARNING TAKING PLACE
• Repetition of 'at' words. • Copying labels from the environment which she can read.	• Returns to written language she feels safe with: 'at' words and print in the environment which she can read. • Writing must be able to be read and have meaning.

Sample 4: June

Background

At the beginning of this writing session the teacher had shown the children the rhyme, 'I'm a Witch', in the written form. The children had learnt this rhyme previously and now 'read' the words which the teacher had written on large sheets of cardboard. The teacher pointed to each word as the children 'read' the rhyme. They worked out what word said 'witch', what word said 'hat' and so on. The teacher suggested to the children that they might like to write about the witch in the writing session.

Descriptive Account of the Process

Lam drew a house, grass, sun, and then a tractor and a witch. He wrote his name, then the line of letters beginning with 'LG'. When the teacher came to talk to him about his piece, he explained there was no driver in the tractor because the witch had taken him away.

He began to 'read' his writing: 'The witch take the driver and the tractor . . .' He stopped at the end of the row of letters and, instead of returning to the beginning of the row as he had been doing, he looked at the teacher and said, 'More words.'

'Yes,' said his teacher, 'You need more words.'

Lam picked up his pencil and wrote the letters along the top row, then the letters along the bottom row. He 'read' his writing again.

'The witch take the driver and the tractor go smash in the house and crash the house down. Naughty witch.'

Sample 4: March 3rd

Background

The children had settled well into their Kindergarten class and were beginning to make friends. On this day Sarah and the other children on her table seemed to be in a 'silly' boisterous mood. The teacher had been demonstrating 'how to read' to the children by reading Big Books and things she had written on the board. She demonstrated how to work out unknown words in the text by guessing what the word might be and then confirming it by looking at the sounds in the word.

Sarah

Hipp
HaH
ET
et
cat
Loyll
at
Fan
yam
Im
boy
girl

box

cheese

Descriptive Account of the Process

Sarah wrote her name in the top left corner. She and Ryan then began making meaningless noises like 'yip', 'fip', 'hip', 'har', and then long sequences of sounds like 'yip, yip, yip; hip, hip, hip.' Sarah announced: 'I'll write "hip" and "har".' She carefully sounded out aloud 'huh-i-puh' and wrote 'Hipp'. She sounded out 'huh-ar' and wrote 'HaH'. She wrote these under each other in a column.

She then announced: 'I'm going to write "ET" the big way and the little way.'

She wrote 'ET' and 'et' and went on to 'cat', 'Loyll' and 'at'—all written under each other.

Ryan asked, 'How do you write "fan"?'

'Fuh-a-n,' Sarah replied. She wrote it on her paper and Ryan copied it, noting 'That's in my name,' and pointing to the 'n'.

Ryan and Sarah began the noise game again: 'Fan, fan, fan, yam, yam, yam'.

Sarah sounded out 'yuh-a-m' and wrote 'yam'.

She then copied 'I'm, 'boy', 'girl'' from the labels on the wall. Next she drew a box and labelled it 'box'. She then drew some cheese and asked the teacher to write the appropriate label underneath it. The teacher wrote 'cheese'.

Comments

Lam seems to have engaged with the teacher's opening demonstration of one-to-one correspondence when reading words. His realisation that he needed to write 'more words' rather than return to the beginning of the row is a response to that demonstration. He seems to be beginning all his 'writing' now with LG, though he is still using the coping strategy of copying random letters. He also still draws first, but then writes without being asked to. He is beginning to experiment with a new hypothesis: the length of a story depends on the amount of 'words' in it.

COPING STRATEGIES BEING USED	LANGUAGE LEARNING TAKING PLACE
• Using related activity—drawing. • Copying random letters and placing meaning on them.	• Beginning to realise the length of a story depends on the amount of words/letters. • Using the language of written language—'word, letters, read, write'.

Sample 5: August

Background

Lam and his friends were still speaking to each other in Vietnamese, but when the teacher came near them or sat at their table they spoke only in English. Their English linguistic data pool was growing. The teacher had begun this session by reading 'Three Billy Goats Gruff' to the class.

Comments

Despite the demonstrations in books and on charts and labels Sarah is persisting with repetition of the column format. She is also using repetition of known words (ET and 'at' words) and copying known labels. But there is also evidence of new hypothesis testing being tried out. Sarah is writing temporary spellings by sounding out (phonemic segmentation). This is a new coping strategy she is trying, viz. trying to write unknown, and in this case, 'nonsense' words. It is significant to remember that the teacher has been demonstrating 'sounding out' during reading sessions.

COPING STRATEGIES BEING USED	LANGUAGE LEARNING TAKING PLACE
• Repetition. • Using temporary spelling. • Interacting with peers.	• Beginning to understand the sound-symbol system of written language. • Uses 'sounding out' to make nonsense words. • Testing her knowledge with peers. • Can read her own written text.

Sample 5: March 10th

Background

When someone has a birthday in the class, they come to the front of the class, bend over and get one smack on the bottom, gently given, for each year. On this particular morning a visitor to the room, Mr Stone, admitted it was his birthday and much to the delight of the children he was submitted to the 'birthday treatment'.

Sarah

This morning Yesterday Mr Ston Stephen got Birthday got When Smacs got Birthday this morning Smacs FElicity got Birthday Smacs

Descriptive Account of the Process

Lam first drew a car, then the house, announcing as he was drawing, 'I do Three Bears' house.' He drew the little stick figure near the house. 'Goldilocks,' he said. Then he drew the three stick figures, saying, 'No, I not do Three Bears' house. I do my dad, my mum and my tall sister.' He started writing: txH. He stopped.

TEACHER:	What are you writing?
LAM:	The Goldilocks is going to the Three Bears' house. (*He continues to write.*) Look I write 'is'.
TEACHER:	How did you know how to write 'is'?
LAM:	(*pointing to the chart 'This is Father Bear'*) Up there.
TEACHER:	What does your writing say?
LAM:	(*slowly*) The Goldilocks is going to the Three Bears' house.
TEACHER:	What is the next word you are going to write?
LAM:	'Going'.
TEACHER:	What does 'going' start with?
TRUNG:	Guh, guh. Like this. (*He points to the 'g' in his name.*)
LAM:	(*writes 'g' and then writes a letter for each word he says: to [Q], the [r], Three Bears' [F]*) House. How do you write house?
TRUNG:	Huh, huh.

Lam wrote 'R'. He then wrote a whole string of letters which he ignored in reading back. He drew a line around the first group of letters, and another around the second set of letters. When asked why, he replied, 'I write a long word.'

Comments

Lam is using a range of coping strategies now. He still draws first and then writes random sets of letters (each letter being a place-holder for a word). But he is beginning to use temporary spellings. He copies 'is' from a chart on the wall. He is also beginning to seek assistance from his peers, and becoming more aware of such terms as 'words, letters, start with, read, write'.

COPING STRATEGIES BEING USED	LANGUAGE LEARNING TAKING PLACE
• Using related activity—drawing. • Copying random letters and placing meaning on them. • Copying words for a specific purpose. • Using peer assistance.	• Understanding of 'one word written for one word said'. • Developing written language concepts—'long words'.

Descriptive Account of the Process

Sarah decided to write about Mr Stone getting birthday smacks. She wrote her name in the usual top left-hand corner. She copied from environmental print 'This morning'. 'This' needed one glance, 'morning' needed three. She found 'Mr' from the Mr Men books in the library and began a new line with 'Mr'. She then looked all around the room for the word 'Stone'. She couldn't find it, so she began to sound it out audibly: 'S-tuh-o-n'. As she sounded each letter she looked at the alphabet chart on the wall to check how to write the letter.

Next she wrote 'got' without seeming to scrounge it from environmental print, and so she must have known it from memory. 'Birthday' was copied from the 'Birthday Chart'. Finally she sounded out 'smacks' using her new phonemic strategy. In the next sentence she copied 'this' and 'morning' from her first writing of them. She then asked Felicity how to spell her name. Felicity pointed to her name tag and spelt it out as Sarah wrote it. 'Got' was written from memory and 'Birthday' and 'smacs' were copied from the sentence above. In the next sentence she used the same strategies. When she had finished, she could read her piece back and recognise individual words.

Comments

Sarah seems to have abandoned the safety net of her 'at' words and the writing in single columns. She is beginning to demonstrate an understanding of writing a meaningful message which hasn't been displayed before. She is beginning to experiment with left-to-right setting out but still hasn't got it quite right. Each sentence is written in its own 'space'. Sarah has not yet tackled the conventions of when upper or lower case letters are used, but tends to copy them as they are written in the sources she uses.

COPING STRATEGIES BEING USED	LANGUAGE LEARNING TAKING PLACE
• Copying from environmental print. • Using temporary spelling. • Assistance from peers.	• Beginning to draw on various sources to write a desired message. (What do I know from memory? What can I scrounge from around me? What will I have a go at?) • Now writing from personal experience—an observation/recount.

Sample 6: September

Background

Lam had been ill and away from school for two weeks. Many children were now copying labels from around the room. Some were writing temporary spellings. The children had been given 'Writing Books'—five sheets of paper stapled together. Lam seemed to be quieter and relied on his Vietnamese friends during this session.

Descriptive Account of the Process

Lam wrote his name first on the top left-hand corner. He then wrote 'L H' but crossed it out. He went and got a card out of a box which had a lion on it with the word 'lion' written underneath. He placed this under his piece of paper and traced the shape of the lion. He wrote 'Lion'. He repeated these actions for the card with a kangaroo on it and then drew lines down the page. When he'd finished he took it over to his teacher to read to her.

LAM:	I read now?
TEACHER:	Yes, good Lam.
LAM:	(*touching the appropriate word*) Lion, kangaroo.
TEACHER:	What is the drawing about?
LAM:	The kangaroo and the lion are in the zoo.

Sample 6: March 31st

Background

During each writing session there was by now a great deal of 'talk' about writing. Children would ask each other 'How do you write . . . ?' Children also knew that they could get up and go to various sources around the room, including other children, in search of words they needed. They would also often share their writing with other children in the room. Sarah was beginning to take books from the class library which she read with confidence. Although she was not always quite correct in the words she read, she was getting the main message of the text.

Sarah
The cat Book The cat climupThe
benstrec He went to School I
did Sum Speling Homewok
Theen I did Sum Marts
and did Sum rods.

Descriptive Account of the Process

Sarah wrote her name and then wrote quickly and with apparent confidence, pausing only now and then to scrounge a word from the environment or sound it out audibly. The following words were written from memory: the, cat, book, up, he, went, to, I, and. These were scrounged from the environment: school, homework, rods, did. The following were approximated using a phonemic strategy: benstrec (beanstalk), sum (some), speling (spelling). And these words appeared to be retrieved from visual memory but not in conventional form: theen (then), marts (maths). Sarah could read her piece, although she balked at 'beanstalk' and 'I'.

Comment

Sarah has abandoned her column format. This is the first piece where her writing goes all the way across the page, left to right. As well as her established strategies she is beginning to use another one in spelling: 'spelling the way I think it looks'. It could now be posited that Sarah is beginning to read because she is now able to retrieve words that she has

Comments

Lam is using the coping strategy of copying a picture and its appropriate word, which he then reads. When asked why he had crossed out the 'LH' in the corner of his work, he said that he'd made a mistake. It seems he is now aware that there is a particular way of writing words in English and he is only going to write those he knows. We know he can hear the beginning sounds of words, but he is reluctant to take a risk and 'have a go' at temporary spellings.

COPING STRATEGIES BEING USED	LANGUAGE LEARNING TAKING PLACE
• Copying words from the environment that he can read.	• A 'word' says something (lion) and that word is always written the same way. • Random letters don't really say anything. • Realises he can 'read' labels in the environment.

Sample 7: October

Background

Lam was still sitting with Doan in the writing sessions and they often chatted to each other in Vietnamese. There had been a wild hailstorm the week before and both children had been amazed at the 'iceblocks' that fell from the sky. This episode was being drawn repeatedly in their work.

seen. Although she is hearing stories read to her and is reading for herself, her attempts at writing a narrative (i.e. a story) are still not conventional. In this piece she begins with a narrative form: 'The cat book. The cat climbed up the beanstalk. He went to school.' But then she moves into writing a comment about her own personal experience of what she did at school.

COPING STRATEGIES BEING USED	LANGUAGE LEARNING TAKING PLACE
• Copying from environment for a specific purpose. • Using temporary spelling.	• Beginning to write across the page. • Beginning to leave spaces between words. • Beginning to use spelling strategy—'spelling as it looks'. • Beginning to read. • Can write a recount, comment, observation, and beginning to write narrative.

Sample 7: April 4th

Background
The writing sessions appeared to be very 'busy'. The teacher had begun to 'publish' some children's writing, which was shared with the class at the beginning of the session.

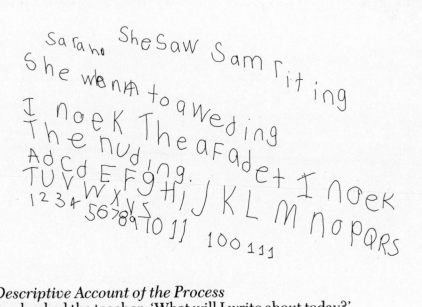

Descriptive Account of the Process
Sarah asked the teacher: 'What will I write about today?'
    'Anything interesting happened at home?' she replied.

Descriptive Account of the Process
A great deal of talk in Vietnamese went on whilst Lam drew this picture.
He told his teacher that he was talking to Doan about coming to play at
her house, which is what the drawing is about. He also pointed out that
'the sun is out but a cloud is coming and the ice balls fall from the sky and
it rain.'

When asked where he would write he replied, 'I can't write'.

Comments
Lam, it seems, has become very reluctant to have a go at writing. For two
weeks now he has drawn without writing any letters or copying any
words from around the room. He copies ideas for his drawings from
Doan. His teacher comments that he watches very carefully when they
write as a class, and that he can identify beginning sounds but is unsure
of how to write many of them. It seems that Lam is coping by using a
related activity but is reluctant to have a go at temporary spellings. He
has become aware that words are written in a certain way and he is not
yet prepared to take the risk of being wrong. Because of the setting
within which he finds himself, he knows he can mark time whilst he
gathers more information about written language from around him. He
knows his drawings will be accepted until the time comes when he feels
confident and competent enough to begin to have a go at English
spellings.

COPING STRATEGIES BEING USED	LANGUAGE LEARNING TAKING PLACE
• Using related activity—drawing. • Repetition of items in drawing.	• Identifying beginning sounds in words but reluctant to have a go at writing them. • Marking time while gathering more information about written language.

'Yes, my mum went to a wedding. I'll write about that.'

Sarah began by writing her name in the usual place. Then she wrote, left to right across the page: 'She whnn to a weding'.

Sarah wrote 'she', 'whnn', 'to' and 'a' from memory. She sounded out 'wed' and copied 'ing' from a word on a chart. When she read it back she realised she had made an error: 'That says "when" not "went".' She found 'went' from environmental print and copied it over 'when'.

'Before she went she got some writing,' she remarked.

'You mean an invitation?' asked the teacher.

'Yes, I better tell that.'

She then wrote above the first sentence: 'she saw sam riting'. She wrote 'she' from memory, copied 'saw' from the environment, sounded out 'some' and 'rit' and copied 'ing'.

Sarah then wrote what appeared to be a completely new piece:

I noek The aFadet I noek The nuding

Adcd . . . etc

123 . . . etc.

She read this back without hesitation: 'I know the alphabet and I know the numbers.'

Comments

Sarah seems to be in control of the strategies with which she has been experimenting. Her spelling of 'know' as 'noek' confirms her experimentation with the 'spelling as it looks' strategy and further supports evidence that she is beginning to 'read like a writer'. She is becoming sensitive to demonstrations of graphic shapes while engaged in reading. When asked why she spelled 'noek' with a 'k' she replied: 'I saw it in a book and I know it's got a "k" in it somewhere.'

Her sense of story has not yet shown any development, as the pieces she writes are brief and cryptic. In this piece she has both a recount (about her mother going to the wedding) and a comment about how she can write letters and the alphabet. Both emanate from her personal experience. But when she had asked what she should write about, the teacher had replied 'Anything happen at home?' and Sarah had responded to this question. She did realise that the second sentence she wrote about her mother receiving the invitation needed to come before telling her audience that her mother went to the wedding. This adding of new information can be viewed as editing.

COPING STRATEGIES BEING USED	LANGUAGE LEARNING TAKING PLACE
• Copying from environment for a specific purpose. • Using temporary spelling. • Seeking assistance from the teacher.	• Developing understanding of the need for sufficient information for her audience. • Experimenting with editing. • Using 'spelling as it looks'.

Sample 8: November

Background
The teacher had made a conscious effort to sit with Lam at least once a week to assist him in his attempts to 'sound out' words.

Descriptive Account of the Process
Lam drew himself sitting on a chair. He then wrote his name beside himself. (He writes this now from memory and in fact no longer has a name card.) He then wrote 'TVT' for 'chair'. The 'T' sound was the closest he could find to the 'ch' in 'chair'. He then drew a cow and, sounding the word slowly, wrote 'kw'. Next he drew 'three houses for mouses'. He then wrote 'ms' for mouse and a large 'h' for house. He needed the teacher's approval for each of these before he went onto the next thing—for example:

LAM:	Now I write 'cow'. (*He draws a cow.*) How do you write 'c-uh', 'c-uh'? (*He writes 'k'.*) Is that 'c-uh'?
TEACHER:	Yes, that is the letter 'k' and it makes a 'c-uh' sound.
LAM:	C-o-w. W, w, like this? (*He writes 'w'.*)
TEACHER:	Yes, good. What else can you write?

Sample 8: May 27th

Background
The teacher was concerned that the children were not attempting to write narrative. She had been reading many stories to them but so far none seemed to be appearing in their writing. So during this week the teacher talked about the retelling of known stories and demonstrated this by writing a retelling of 'The Three Bears' on the chalkboard. She then suggested to the children that they might like to try doing something similar. Sarah began to write 'Cinderella' the very next day. She took four days to write the piece. What is shown here is the first of two pages.

Sarah 27-5

Wons apon a Time
Theer livd a glrl namd
Cindrela bcoz She had
Some Sinds She had to
agli Step sissders and
hre mum and dad did
Theer one day The door
opend and one oz The
Sans came toThe door
The Sans Sed how e wood
You ulike to come tothe ball
and cindarela Sed can
I come Sed Cindarela
the agli Stepsistaes
Sed no You haveent
got enie nice
dressrs Cindarella
Sed yes I have
got nice drsseas
She had to do
all the Jobs
inthe house
Cindarella
Crid and Crid
and wen She
Wos criing
a feri Sed fech
me a ramcin
So Cindarella
ferht a rarich

Comment

Lam is using the coping strategy of seeking assistance from the teacher as well as using temporary spellings. At this stage he will not take the risk and have a go without the assistance of the teacher, although he is prepared to help Doan when she asks 'how do you write' questions. He has, however, made quite a step from the last month when he appeared to have regressed. But what Lam is attempting this month demonstrates that he hadn't regressed but was more likely gathering information from the many demonstrations of written language around him. He has been adding a great deal of English to his personal linguistic data pool and forming new hypotheses about how to solve the written language puzzle. Until he has gained sufficient information and feels confident about it, he doesn't seem prepared to take the risk of being wrong. In the meantime his level of competency and proficiency in oral English has risen dramatically.

COPING STRATEGIES BEING USED	LANGUAGE LEARNING TAKING PLACE
• Using related activity—drawing items he can say and write. • Using temporary spelling. • Seeking advice from teacher/peers.	• Beginning to use phonemic segmentation. • Can match the graphic symbol to the sound. • Concept of a word/labels. • Beginning to read print in environment.

General comments on Lam's development after 9 months at school

Lam has not turned six, yet he speaks Vietnamese fluently and is becoming increasingly more competent and proficient in English. He is learning to speak, read and write in English all at the same time, although his oral language development is far in advance of his written language. In order to solve the written language puzzle in English, Lam uses various coping strategies. He not only chooses which strategy to use and when to use it, but also how long to use it. The setting in which he finds himself offers him immersion and demonstration in oral and written language and the expectation that he will learn to speak, read and write English. It allows him to take responsibility for pacing this learning, whilst at the same time providing him with daily opportunities to practise speaking, reading and writing in non-threatening situations. Approximations are accepted and indeed rewarded, and constructive

Descriptive Account of the Process
Sarah began this piece confidently. She sometimes paused to scrounge for words around the room but she mainly sounded them out or wrote from memory. She stopped often to reread in order to write on. She talked to the children beside her and read parts of her piece to them.

Comment
Sarah has a repertoire of strategies she now uses to help her to write: using environmental print for a specific purpose; seeking assistance when needed and using temporary spellings. She is continually testing, rejecting, refining, consolidating and extending new and old hypotheses about how writing is done. She is also able to use the appropriate language for the appropriate text, viz. book language: 'once upon a time, cried and cried, fetch a pumpkin.'

COPING STRATEGIES BEING USED	LANGUAGE LEARNING TAKING PLACE
• Using temporary spelling. • Seeking advice from/interacting with peers and teacher. • Copying from the environment for a specific purpose.	• Responding to request for a specific type of writing: retelling known story. • Writing over several days. • Using a variety of spelling strategies. • Using language appropriate to type of writing—'once upon a time', 'cried and cried'.

General comments on Sarah's development after 12 weeks at school

From her very first piece it was evident that Sarah came to school with quite a deal of knowledge of written language. This knowledge has increased rapidly within the first twelve weeks of school. Sarah has had the opportunity to try new hypotheses about the written language puzzle. She has been immersed in a print-oriented classroom which has given her countless demonstrations of written language. Her teacher has given her both the time and the responsibility to experiment with writing. The feedback she receives from the teacher and her peers guides her on to further learning. In the twelve-week period Sarah has learnt that:

i)   writing proceeds from left to right across the page
ii)   words have spaces between them

feedback is constantly given where needed. He makes the decision as to when to take the risk of having a go. In the nine months Lam has learnt:

i) spoken English—he can communicate about most things he wants in school
ii) English script
iii) writing proceeds from left to right
iv) writing is for reading and printed words always say the same thing—labels, stories
v) there are letters and words in writing
vi) there are conventional ways to write English words which need to be followed
vii) there are various ways of meeting these conventions, including
  • using the print around the room
  • phonemic segmentation.

iii) lines proceed from top to bottom of pages
iv) stories occur as a sequence of events and the temporal order of these events must be adhered to
v) there are conventions of spelling which need to be followed
vi) there are various ways of meeting these conventions, including:
- visual memory
- using environmental sources until the convention is internalised
- phonemic segmentation.

CHAPTER FIVE

What it all Means for Teaching

We ask again the question from the first chapter: 'Is the reality of these classrooms the "chaos" they appear?' The answer is obviously 'No!' What we have demonstrated in this book is that these 'process-oriented' classrooms are highly structured, organised and robust learning settings. They are classrooms in which certain conditions exist that coerce young learners to develop their own set of strategies to solve the written language puzzle in the ways which best suit their personal needs (i.e. their personal linguistic data pools).

We want now to outline some implications which teachers need to consider in three areas: the classroom setting, the understanding of children's learning and the understanding of the nature of language.

1 The classroom setting

Teachers need to establish classroom settings which allow the conditions outlined on p.7 to be present and to operate at an optimal level. From our observations this happens when teachers do the following.

Immersion

Teachers surround their children with print—a wide variety of print—including labels on the art and craft work around the room; labels on items in the room; charts; commercially produced books and books written by the children. It is important for the children to feel a sense of ownership of this print, and so teachers write the labels and charts with the children, ensuring that the print is always meaningful to them. The print changes from time to time as various themes are dealt with in the classroom.

Children are also immersed in a great deal of oral language. The talking, listening, reading and writing encounters give children opportunities to 'fill' their personal linguistic data pools.

Demonstrations

There are many opportunities in these classrooms for demonstrations of how language and print work. When teachers write a label in front of the children to go alongside the latest craft work, they are demonstrating how writing works. When teachers write their own piece in front of their children, thinking aloud as they search for what they want to say and how to spell the words, and as they check the punctuation, they are demonstrating how drafts are written, how to edit, how to deal with unknown spellings, and how to use the environment to scrounge for words. They are also demonstrating how they read over their writing to check for meaning, and how to rewrite the piece so that it can 'go public' for all to read.

The way teachers approach reading and writing demonstrates their attitude towards literacy: whether they like to read and write; whether they think reading and writing are hard or easy, enjoyable or a chore.

Shared Book Experience is a method teachers use to demonstrate much about written language and how it is read: what punctuation marks are for; how words are spelt; what to do when you can't read a word; what sound the various symbols make, and so on. By reading daily to children teachers demonstrate the value of reading and how enjoyable it can be. By reading informational books as well as story books, they demonstrate that books are written for a variety of purposes and about a variety of topics.

Teachers demonstrate that they expect children to learn to read and write by allocating valuable school time for reading and writing. Most importantly, they are constantly demonstrating how reading, writing and spelling are interrelated.

Responsibility

(There are many interpretations and misinterpretations of this term. By responsibility we simply mean 'making decisions for oneself about learning'.) Teachers organise their classrooms and activities in such a way that the children must take responsibility for many of the decisions about their learning: for instance, what book will I read? What topic will I write about? Which piece of writing will I edit and publish? Which book or part of the book will I share with the group? Is there something I can do as a follow-up to the book I've read? Where do I find that word I need? What part of the written language puzzle will I learn next?

Teachers take responsibility for the organisation of the overall program; for selecting a wide range of books and other printed materials; for providing adequate paper, pens and other materials for writing; for the way time is used in the classroom; for knowing how each child is developing; for supporting and teaching each child at the point of need; for keeping records of each child's progress.

While young learners are encouraged and expected to make many decisions about their learning, they cannot be expected to make them all. There are many decisions made by the teacher which are simply non-negotiable. For example, teachers take the responsibility that children will write and read in the time allocated to writing and reading. They will work within the rules of operation established by the teacher with them.

However, the teachers we have observed try to keep a balance of who is responsible for what. For example, they view scribing for children as a form of publishing rather than writing on behalf of the child, and so children have a go at writing before the teacher steps in. They do not give children spellings unless they have first made some attempt of their own. They do not always select the books that the children read. They allow children to choose from a range of activities (though of course the range of choice represents some decision-making on behalf of the child). By being encouraged to seek out information for themselves and make some decisions about their learning for themselves, children become less reliant on the teacher. They become independent learners who can make decisions for themselves.

Expectations

Teachers expect their children to learn. They expect them to take responsibility for decisions about their learning. They expect their children to have a go at spelling the words they need; to have a go at the words they don't know in their reading; to be able to choose their own topics in writing and choose their own books in reading. They expect their children to carry out their tasks sensibly at an agreed level of quality that both child and teacher accept. These expectations are worked out in consultation with the children, so that everyone knows what is expected of them within the classroom setting.

Expectations are also communicated in the ways that teachers treat their children. They realise they must be careful not to communicate that certain tasks are achievable by some children and not others. Thus they avoid grouping children in ability groups, but encourage co-operative learning in flexible groups.

Children expect what they do in the name of language learning to be meaningful. They learned to speak without being 'taught'. It was simply learned as they used talk to achieve various purposes in their lives. Why then should they expect anything different when learning to read and write?

Approximations

Teachers encourage children to have a go. They do not expect children's attempts to be perfect first time around. They understand that learning occurs only when learners have opportunities to gather new information and formulate hypotheses about written language, which then need to be trialled and tested before becoming part of the learners' repertoire. Children need to know they can try out these hypotheses and make mistakes, and that their approximations will be accepted, for only then will they be prepared to take risks and experiment in their learning.

Practice

Teachers provide time for children to read and write, which they fill with activities that cannot be completed unless reading, writing, talking and listening are all involved. However, these activities have other purposes and functions besides learning about language, and whatever is learned about language is a by-product of the uses to which reading, writing, talking and listening are put. For example, the purpose of reading a book may be simply personal enjoyment or to convince one's peers that it is a great (or boring) book.

This classroom setting gives children plenty of opportunity to read and to share their reading.

Response

Teachers interact with their children about their reading and writing attempts in such a way that the type of feedback is both supportive and instructive to the young learner. (Teachers also encourage children to respond to each other's work in a similar way.) The interaction may take the form of a class lesson, a group activity or a one-to-one conference. But whatever form it takes, the response always emanates from the perceived needs of the child or children. The teachers learn about what they need to teach from observing and listening to their children.

2 Understanding children's learning

Teachers should be aware of the coping strategies their children use and know why they are using them. The strategies we've outlined in Chapter Two will help teachers understand what they observe as their children are attempting to solve the written language puzzle. Teachers also need to understand why children like Lam need to use some strategies for longer periods of time than children like Sarah.

They need to support their children in the use of their coping strategies, whilst at the same time gently encouraging them to try new ways of doing things. For example, if teachers observe that some children are not using temporary spelling, they need to ask themselves several questions. Is it because of the demonstrations given to the children, or lack of them? Would more explicit demonstrations of working out how to spell a word be useful? Would individual alphabet charts assist? . . . and so on.

3 Understanding the nature of language

Teachers need to understand how reading, writing, talking and listening are interrelated. The notion of the linguistic data pool, we believe, assists teachers in seeing how this relationship operates. One consequence is that classroom programming in the traditional sense has to change: programming under 'Reading', 'Writing', 'Talking' and 'Listening' headings becomes obsolete. Rather, teachers need to organise activities in their classrooms which encourage children to mingle reading, writing, talking and listening. Whilst the main focus of an activity may be, for instance, on reading, that doesn't exclude opportunities for talking, listening and writing taking place as well.

Teachers also need to encourage co-operative learning rather than competitive learning. Peer support and tutoring has been demonstrated as a very useful strategy for learning.

゜   ゜   ゜

Overall, what has been written in this book means that teachers need to consider quite a different set of beliefs about how young learners solve the written language puzzle. And we maintain that if teachers take the opportunity to observe their children in action, they will validate from their own observations and data what we have written. They will then know *why* their children follow the learning path that they choose to take. They will be better armed to support and instruct the young learners in their care. Classrooms will be settings where teachers have confidence in what they are doing and trust that their children *are* learning.

References

Bissex, G. (1980), *Gnys at Wrk: A Child Learns to Read and Write*, Harvard University Press, Cambridge, Mass.

Bouffler, C. (1984), 'Spelling as a language process', *in* Unsworth, L. (ed.), *Reading, Writing and Spelling*, Proceedings of the Fifth Macarthur Reading/Language Symposium, Sydney.

Butler, A. & Turbill, J. (1984), *Towards a Reading-Writing Classroom*, Primary English Teaching Association, Rozelle.

Cambourne, B. et al. (1984), *Process Writing in English Speaking and Non-English Speaking Background Kindergarten Classes: A Report on Research in Progress*, Monograph, Centre for Studies in Literacy, Wollongong University, Wollongong.

Cambourne, B. (1986), 'Process writing and non-English speaking background children', *Australian Reading Journal*, **9**,3, 126–37.

Crafton, L. (1983), 'Oral and written language: related processes of a sociopsycholinguistic nature', *in* Hardt, U.H. (ed.) *Teaching Reading with the Other Language Arts*, International Reading Association, Newark.

Dyson, A.H. (1982), 'Reading, writing and language: young children solving the written language puzzle', *Language Arts*, **59**,8, 829–39.

Ferreiro, E. & Teberosky, A. (1982), *Literacy before Schooling*, Heinemann Educational Books, Exeter, New Hampshire.

Graves, D. (1983), *Writing: Teachers and Children at Work*, Heinemann Educational Books, Exeter, New Hampshire.

Harste, J.C., Woodward, V.A. & Burke, C.L. (1984), *Language Stories and Literacy Lessons*, Heinemann Educational Books, Exeter, New Hampshire.

Read, C. (1974), 'Pre-school children's knowledge of English phonology', *Harvard Educational Review*, **41**,1, 1–34.

Smith, F. (1981), *Writing and the Writer*, Holt, Rinehart & Winston, New York.

Turbill, J. (1982), *No Better Way to Teach Writing*, Primary English Teaching Association, Rozelle.

Turbill, J. (1983), *Now, We Want to Write*, Primary English Teaching Association, Rozelle.

Walshe, R. (1981), *Donald Graves in Australia: Children Want to Write*, Primary English Teaching Association, Rozelle.